# WENSLEYDALE

## HILLSIDE GUIDES

**LONG DISTANCE WALKS**
- 1 • THE WESTMORLAND WAY
- 2 • THE FURNESS WAY
- 3 • THE CUMBERLAND WAY
- 7 • CLEVELAND WAY COMPANION
- 9 • THE NORTH BOWLAND TRAVERSE
  (by David Johnson)
- 16 • DALES WAY COMPANION
- 22 • THE COAST TO COAST WALK

**CIRCULAR WALKS - YORKSHIRE DALES**
- 4 • WALKS IN WHARFEDALE
- 5 • WALKS IN NIDDERDALE
- 6 • WALKS IN THE CRAVEN DALES
- 8 • WALKS IN WENSLEYDALE
- 10 • WALKS IN THREE PEAKS COUNTRY
- 11 • WALKS IN SWALEDALE
- 20 • RAMBLES IN WHARFEDALE
- 21 • WALKS ON THE HOWGILL FELLS

**CIRCULAR WALKS - NORTH YORK MOORS**
- 13 • WESTERN - Cleveland/Hambleton Hills
- 14 • SOUTHERN - Rosedale/Farndale/Bransdale
- 15 • NORTHERN - Eskdale and the Coast

**CIRCULAR WALKS - SOUTH PENNINES**
- 12 • WALKS IN BRONTE COUNTRY
- 17 • WALKS IN CALDERDALE

**HILLWALKING - LAKE DISTRICT**
- 18 • OVER LAKELAND MOUNTAINS
- 19 • OVER LAKELAND FELLS

---

**FREEDOM OF THE DALES**
40 selected walks
*Full colour hardback*

---

**80 DALES WALKS**
Omnibus edition of Books 4,6,8,11 and (in part)10,21
*Published by Cordee, Leicester*

# WALKS
## IN
# WENSLEYDALE

## by

## Paul Hannon

HILLSIDE PUBLICATIONS

HILLSIDE PUBLICATIONS
11 Nessfield Grove
Exley Head
Keighley
West Yorkshire
BD22 6NU


First published 1987
5th (revised) impression 1992

TO MY PARENTS
and my first Wensleydale memory,
of our fish and chips in Hawes


Page 1 illustration: On Penhill End


The maps in this book are based upon
the 1914-30 Ordnance Survey 1:10,560 maps

ISBN 1 870141 16 4


Printed in Great Britain by
Carnmor Print and Design
95/97 London Road
Preston
Lancashire
PR1 4BA

# INTRODUCTION

Wensleydale is a broad green valley with innumerable hidden features that more than make amends for its lack of instant grandeur. Here one must make an effort to seek out the attractions, and the ensuing pages lead the discerning walker to a host of splendid sights. An oft-made claim that this is Yorkshire's major dale is a point that Wharfedale would surely debate, unless the many side-valleys and the fertile pastures downstream of the National Park boundary are included. These lesser valleys are something unique to Wensleydale, for Coverdale, Walden, Bishopdale, Raydale and several more are all sizeable dales in their own right. Each contributes its share to the Wensleydale scene.

The individuality of the valley is also exhibited by its very name - this is the only major dale not to take its title from its river. The Ure — anciently the Yore, a name still applied in some quarters - lost out to the village of Wensley which lies just outside the Park on the road to Middleham. This the Dales' most fertile valley was once a great hunting forest, and other associations with history involve a Brigantes' hill-fort, Iron-age lake-dwellings, a Roman road, a Roman fort, a 13th century abbey, a 14th century castle, a 15th century fortified manor-house, a 16th century beacon-site, a 17th century hall, and traces of lead and coal-mining and of quarrying. Not bad for starters!

The natural attractions surely deserve a mention now. It will be noticed that not many walks take in the riverbank, for a good deal of its course is without rights-of-way: the river itself leads an uneventful life other than one or two famous moments which all who have visited the dale will already know. Neither are the high tops very inviting, indeed the bulk of Wensleydale's walking is to be had somewhere between the two extremities. The physical structure of the dale gives us a series of regular ledges on which some superb walking can be found. These mid-height terraces also generally provide the best views.

The crowning glory of Wensleydale however (despite the Ure's general lack of interest) are the waterfalls. Nowhere else can boast such a fine array of tumbling falls, for most of the side-valleys also proudly possess their own force. These are the gems that make Wensleydale special.

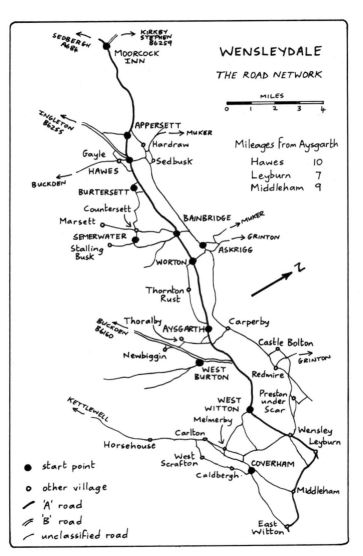

WENSLEYDALE

THE ROAD NETWORK

MILES
0  1  2  3  4

Mileages from Aysgarth

Hawes        10
Leyburn       7
Middleham     9

SEDBERGH A684 →
→ KIRKBY STEPHEN B6259
● MOORCOCK INN

INGLETON B6255 →
APPERSETT
→ MUKER
Hardraw
Gayle
○ Sedbusk
HAWES
BUCKDEN →
BURTERSETT
Countersett
Marsett ○
SEMERWATER
Stalling Busk
BAINBRIDGE → MUKER
→ GRINTON
ASKRIGG
WORTON
Thornton Rust
BUCKDEN B6160 →
Thoralby
AYSGARTH
Carperby
Castle Bolton
→ GRINTON
Newbiggin
WEST BURTON
Redmire
WEST WITTON
Preston under Scar
KETTLEWELL →
Melmerby
Carlton
Wensley
Leyburn
Horsehouse
West Scrafton
Caldbergh
COVERHAM
Middleham
East Witton

● start point
○ other village
╱ 'A' road
╱╱ 'B' road
╱ unclassified road

6

The 16 walks described range from 3½ to 11 miles in length, and the terrain similarly varies from riverside strolls to rather more strenuous moorland walking. All the walks are circular, and with an average distance of 6½ miles are ideally suited to half-day rambles.

Each walk is given its own chapter consisting of an 'immediate impression' diagram, detailed narrative, strip-map, and notes and illustrations of features of interest.

## ORDNANCE SURVEY MAPS

While the strip-maps illustrating each walk should be sufficient to guide one safely around, they are unable to show the surrounding countryside. The remedy is an OS map.

1:50,000 : Landranger sheets 98, 99

1:25,000 : Outdoor Leisure Map 30 – Yorkshire Dales North/Central
This covers all but Walks 8 and 10, which can be found on Pathfinder sheets 608-NY80/SD89 and 617-SD69/79 respectively

*Aysgarth Falls*

Overleaf are listed the various amenities which can be found in the area. Public transport is above average for the Dales, with two services up the dale to Hawes, and a number of other seasonal or infrequent routes. Rail stations are at Northallerton to the east and Garsdale Head to the west.

# SOME USEFUL FACILITIES

| | Accommodation | Inn | Car park | Bus service | Post Office | other shop | Payphone | WC |
|---|---|---|---|---|---|---|---|---|
| Appersett | • | | | • | | | • | |
| Askrigg | • | • | | • | • | • | • | • |
| Aysgarth | • | • | • | • | • | • | • | • |
| Bainbridge | • | | | • | | | • | |
| Burtersett | • | | | | | | • | |
| Carlton | • | • | | • | • | | • | |
| Carperby | • | • | | • | | | • | |
| Castle Bolton | • | | • | | • | | • | • |
| Countersett | • | | | | | | | |
| Coverham | | | | • | | | | |
| Gayle | • | | | • | | | • | |
| Hardraw | • | • | | | | • | • | |
| Hawes | • | • | • | • | • | • | • | • |
| Horsehouse | • | • | | • | • | | • | |
| Thornton Rust | • | | | • | • | | • | |
| West Burton | • | • | | • | • | | • | |
| West Witton | • | • | | • | • | | • | |
| Worton | • | • | | • | | | • | |

Youth hostels can be found at Aysgarth Falls and Hawes.
There are campsites around Hawes – Market day is Tuesday.
This is a general guide only – if it's important, check it!

# SOME USEFUL ADDRESSES

Ramblers' Association
   1/5 Wandsworth Road, London  SW8 2XX
      Tel. 071-582 6878

Youth Hostels Association
   Trevelyan House, St. Albans, Herts. AL1 2DY
      Tel. 0727- 55215

Yorkshire Dales National Park Office
   Colvend, Hebden Road, Grassington,
   Skipton, North Yorkshire BD23 5LB
      Tel. 0756- 752748

Hawes National Park Centre (Station Yard)
   Tel. 0969- 667450

Aysgarth Falls National Park Centre
   Tel. 0969- 663424

Leyburn Tourist Information (Thornborough Hall)
   Tel. 0969 - 23069

Yorkshire and Humberside Tourist Board
   312 Tadcaster Road, York YO2 2HF
      Tel. 0904- 707961

Dales Countryside Museum, Station Yard, Hawes
   Tel. 0969- 667450

Yorkshire Dales Society
   Otley Civic Centre, Cross Green,
   Otley, West Yorkshire LS21 1HD
      Tel. 0943 - 607868

United Automobile Services (buses)
   Grange Road, Darlington, Co. Durham
      Tel. 0325- 468771

Richmondshire District Council publishes an annual
accommodation guide which includes all Wensleydale.
The Tourist Information office is at Friary Gardens,
Richmond, Tel. 0748- 850252.

# THE WALKS

Listed below are the 16 walks described, the walk number being the key to easy location in the guide

# THE WALKS

## Outline map showing the routes and the starting points

- 1 Aysgarth
- 2 Bainbridge
- 3 Hawes
- 4 Coverham
- 5 Worton
- 6 Aysgarth

- 7 Burtersett
- 8 Appersett
- 9 West Witton
- 10 Moorcock Inn
- 11 Hawes
- 12 Askrigg
- 13 West Burton
- 14 West Witton
- 15 Semerwater
- 16 West Burton

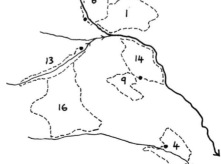

River Ure

N

A log of the walks can be found at the end of the book, along with a key to the individual route-maps

WALK 1    | CASTLE BOLTON AND AYSGARTH FALLS |

7 miles                              from Aysgarth

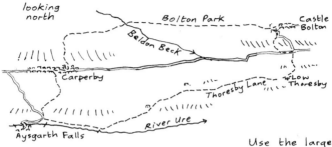

looking
north                    Bolton Park              Castle
                                                   Bolton

                    Beldon Beck

Carperby                              Thoresby Lane      Low
                                                          Thoresby

Aysgarth Falls            River Ure

Visits to two of the valley's
most famous features, one
natural, one the work of man

Use the large
National Park car-
park at Aysgarth
Falls, east of the
village.

| THE WALK |

        From the car park return to the road and turn left
under the old railway bridge. Within a few yards after the
station yard take a hand-gate on the right to enter a wood.
A path rises through the trees, crossing a wide, green path
to a hidden stile just behind. Leaving the wood, bear just
a little right to a stile ahead, from where a string of gap-
stiles point the way half-right through the fields.
        At the last stile turn left to a stile onto the farm
road of Low Lane. Cross straight over it to pass through a
long, narrow field, and from a stile on the right near the
end, continue on to a gate between houses to emerge onto
the road in Carperby, opposite the inn.
        Turn right a short distance and head up the first
lane on the left. This 'no through road' rises out of the
village to become a broad track between walls. Beyond a
barn keep right at a fork to climb by the wall and round
to a gate. A large tract of colourful, rough pasture is
now entered, and with Bolton Castle in view down-dale, our
near-level approach to it can be well surveyed.
        A generally clear green track heads on through

the bracken to arrive at a gate at the far end, then crosses
Beldon Beck and runs a little less clearly along to a gate in
the right-hand wall. From here the track becomes wide and
clear to lead through half a dozen more fields towards the
imposing bulk of Bolton Castle. Through a narrow wood the
track leads to the very walls of the castle.

Between castle and church we emerge onto the
village street alongside the green, and from the corner
it is this road we descend to leave Castle Bolton village.
Soon a track forks right between barns, descending to two
houses and the defunct railway line. Across the old line a
charming, leafy snicket drops down to join a road.

Go left along the road only as far as the Castle
Bolton junction, then take a stile on the right. Cross to
the far end of the field, and from the stile bear right
down to another stile in the very bottom-left corner. It
leads to a small footbridge onto Thoresby Lane. Along
to the right the lane quickly ends at Low Thoresby.

At a gate to the right of the farm the lane is
born again, now as a delectable green byway. Immensely
rewarding throughout its entire hedgerowed length, it finally
terminates just beyond an extremely wet junction. From a stile
into a field follow the wall away to find a stile by a gate at
the very far end. From one behind it follow a wall away to
the next, then bear left over the brow to a stile near the
far corner.

A farm track is joined to lead down to Hollin House,
keeping right at the first building to a gateway before the
barn complex. Take a gap-stile on the left to slant down to
a gate from where a green track heads away: as it swings
down the large field head straight across to a stile. Part-way
along the fence-side drop down left to another stile.

At this point we meet up with the ever-popular
Aysgarth Falls path at its terminus, and just below us
are the Lower Falls. A distinct gap in the cliffs here
permits a cul-de-sac descent to a water's-edge vantage
point. A well trodden path heads up-river, passing by a
short, circular detour to a more intimate viewpoint for
the Lower Falls. Up above the path temporarily vacates
the woodland before entering Freeholder's Wood to quickly
reach the Middle Falls viewing platform. Only yards further
we emerge onto the road just below the car park entrance.

To include the Upper Falls (best seen from Yore Bridge)
turn down the road to gain the bridge, from where a path
then leads directly back up to the car park.

Carperby is one of the most attractive and least spoilt villages in the dale. Its depth is virtually non-existant, for all its sturdy stone dwellings line the road running through the village. Standing well back from the valley bottom, it was once of greater importance as testified by the sizeable market cross. Dating from the seventeenth century it stands at one end of a narrow green. At the opposite end is a good grouping of chapels which have sadly been succumbing to modern trends. It is claimed that the Wensleydale breed of sheep was first named here.

Carperby market cross

Beldon Beck

**Carperby**

kiln

Hargill

inn

ASKRIGG

CASTLE BOLTON

Low Lane

Bolton Castle is a majestic ruin that cannot fail to impress the first-time visitor. When approached from a distance it initially belies its ruinous condition.

Originally a 14th century manor house, it was converted into a castle by Richard, the First Lord Scrope. Mary, Queen of Scots was a famous guest, being imprisoned here from 1568 to 1569.

The castle and its improved facilities are open to visitors, its labyrinth of an interior being well worth exploring. Tea room and gift shop are modern-day essential additions.

Though only the village has the 'Castle' prefixing the 'Bolton' the castle often gets the same treatment.

CARPERBY

Former railway station

National Park Centre

Freeholder's Wood

Hollin House

N

**Aysgarth Falls**

Upper Falls    Middle Falls

R. Ure

Lower Falls

Inn    YH

AYSGARTH VILLAGE A684    WEST WITTON A684

For notes on the Aysgarth area see Walk 6

14

Although comprehensively overshadowed by its castle, the village of Castle Bolton is highly appealing in its own right. A spacious green separates two intermittent rows of cottages, many of which housed the lead-miners of long ago. Today this is a peaceful place, which like Carperby is well up from the valley bottom. The church of St. Oswald stands almost at the castle wall. Dating back more than 600 years, this tiny place of worship reveals a surprisingly spacious interior.

Bolton Park

Bolton Castle

kiln

③

Castle Bolton

REDMIRE

castle

former railway line

CARPERBY

④

ROAD

N

LEYBURN

CASTLE BOLTON

High Thoresby

Thoresby Lane

Watery Lane

wet!

⑤

Low Thoresby (Farm)

Thoresby Lane is a centuries-old byway which feels little altered. Its snaking route between hedgerows is a joy throughout. Watery Lane goes down to ford the Ure: be grateful we don't!

The mighty wall of Penhill is a major feature of the lower dale, and from the environs of Thoresby and Hollin House it is in a particularly dominant mood.

15

WALK 2
5¾ miles

THE RIVER BAIN AND THE ROMAN ROAD

from Bainbridge

A steady ramble by the
shortest river and
along an ancient
highway

Park in the
village centre

looking
south-west

Countersett

Semerwater

River Bain

Bainbridge

THE WALK

Leave Bainbridge by the main road to Aysgarth at the corner of the green, crossing the bridge over the river Bain and climbing the steep hill. Take a stile on the right just before a junction and head across the pasture, keeping well above the steep drop to the river. Pass to the left of an 'island' field and at the brow of the hill a sketchy path leads on to a stile. Marker posts show the way down the slope beyond, with Semerwater now fully in view ahead.

Head on through stiles in the intervening walls, and at a ladder-stile bear right to finally join up with the now adjacent riverbank. Its pleasant course offers a simple walk upstream to quickly arrive at the road at Semerwater Bridge. Before crossing it, have a potter along the lakeshore itself: its foot is directly in front.

To resume the walk, cross the bridge and climb the steep road to the crossroads at Countersett. Turn right for the hamlet, but just before the first house opt instead for an enclosed track to some cottages on the left. Taking a gate by the first dwelling on the left, begin a steep climb to first one and then a second barn. From it rise half-left to a stile and continue diagonally up to the wall rising to the far corner. At this point the Semerwater scene is finally left behind.

From the stile follow the wall up to a gate onto the Countersett-Burtersett road at its highest point. Go right for a couple of minutes to reach a stile on the right. A sketchy path crosses a collapsed wall and then fades in rough pasture as it slants down to a stile onto the Cam High Road.

Turn right to follow the arrow-like course of the Roman road – which is in good 'nick' for its age – until eventual hi-jack by a modern road. Head up this road as far as Gill Edge, just ahead, and turn along its drive. From a stile on the left descend to one at the field-bottom, from where a sketchy path crosses two fields to a barn. A clearer path runs on to two further stiles, and from a gate above the river descends the wallside to the edge of Bainbridge. The path becomes enclosed to run past cottages before re-emerging onto the village green.

---

Bainbridge is a lovely village whose houses stand well back from an enormous green. Though the main road cuts across it, its effect seems insignificant. The most noticeable features are the stocks which still grace the green, and the whitewashed inn which is always in sight. It dates back several centuries and is possibly the oldest in the dale. The structure which gives the village its name is a shapely platform from which to see not only the best stretch of the river, but the only part before it sneaks quietly round the backs of the houses.

The village has notable historical connections, not least of all with the Romans. Brough Hill, peering over the houses at the east of the village, is the site of the Roman fort Braccium and a handy place to defend, which was no doubt just as well. Some centuries later the Norman lords based their foresters here, when the Forest of Wensleydale was a popular hunting-ground. At the inn can be seen a horn, and during the winter months it was blown at nine o'clock in the evening to guide benighted travellers to safety. Its origin goes back earlier still, as a warning sound in the days of the Forest. Happily this ancient event can still sometimes be seen, surviving purely as a quaint custom. Where our walk re-enters

the village is a house that was once the 'Old Dame School', where over a century ago, pupils could learn the 'three R's' for 2d a week (that's 1p to you youngsters!)

the inn from the green

---

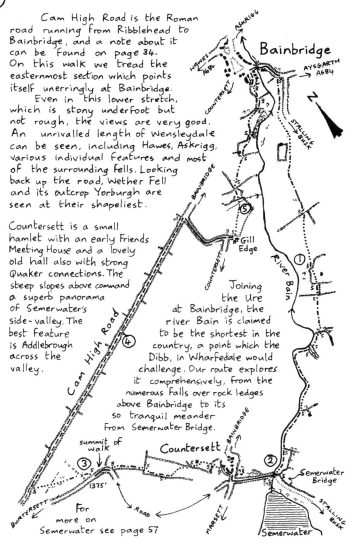

Cam High Road is the Roman road running from Ribblehead to Bainbridge, and a note about it can be found on page 34. On this walk we tread the easternmost section which points itself unerringly at Bainbridge.

Even in this lower stretch, which is stony underfoot but not rough, the views are very good. An unrivalled length of Wensleydale can be seen, including Hawes, Askrigg, various individual features and most of the surrounding fells. Looking back up the road, Wether Fell and its outcrop Yorburgh are seen at their shapeliest.

Countersett is a small hamlet with an early Friends Meeting House and a lovely old hall also with strong Quaker connections. The steep slopes above command a superb panorama of Semerwater's side-valley. The best feature is Addlebrough across the valley.

Joining the Ure at Bainbridge, the river Bain is claimed to be the shortest in the country, a point which the Dibb, in Wharfedale would challenge. Our route explores it comprehensively, from the numerous falls over rock ledges above Bainbridge to its so tranquil meander from Semerwater Bridge.

Bainbridge

AYSGARTH
A684

ASKRIGG

HAWES
A684

COUNTERSETT

STALLING BUSK

River Bain

Gill Edge

COUNTERSETT

BAINBRIDGE

Cam High Road

summit of walk

1375'

BURTERSETT

ROAD

Countersett

BAINBRIDGE

MARSETT

Semerwater Bridge

STALLING BUSK

Semerwater

For more on Semerwater see page 57

WALK 3

## HARDRAW FORCE AND HIGH CLINT

7¼ miles

from Hawes

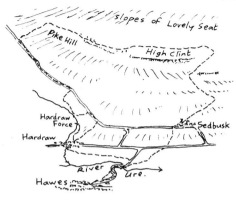

looking north

**A superbly varied walk with extensive views across Wensleydale**

Use the main National Park car-park in the old railway station yard

## THE WALK

From the car park take the path by the old railway bridge up onto the road, and turn right to follow it out of the village. Within a few yards a track heads off to the left, and with it a gate signals the route of the Pennine Way, whose flagged course is followed to rejoin the road a little further on. Cross Haylands Bridge over the Ure, then take a stile which soon appears on the right, a sketchy path going across the field to a small, arched bridge.

From it the path climbs half-right to a stile, from which a large field is crossed to a stile in the top corner. Cross straight over the road to a stile opposite, and resume the rise in the same direction. Two further stiles quickly ensue before a near-vertical climb to another stile in the top-right corner. Turn right along the road to the hamlet of Sedbusk.

Head up the lane between the houses, and at the top end of the small green bear right as the lane deteriorates into a rough track. This is Shutt Lane, which slants up the hillside to be vacated by a stile on the left just before a gate. A good sunken track works its way up the field, passing a tiny plantation and then slanting left to a gate. The track runs on to another gate which gives access to the open fell.

Continue straight up the track keeping left of a low scar, and the way then gives High Clint, on the left, a wide berth before swinging round onto the plateau above it. The track runs along to the far end of the plateau, meeting up there with a more attractive path that has stayed with High Clint's escarpment: a prominent cairn to the left overlooks a splendid grouping of stone men.

Throughout almost all of this walk we are treading the slopes of Lovely Seat, which rises very gradually above us to 2213 feet.

Back on the track, a left fork is passed and the way quickly peters out. Forge straight on to another series of cairns on Pike Hill, and maintain a level course to arrive at the lively environs of Shivery Gill. Cross to a track on the other side and turn down it to join the unfenced Buttertubs road, which is now followed downhill for a good mile and a quarter.

At the first farm buildings at High Shaw turn along the lane on the right, only to leave it after a few yards by descending steps to heavily wooded Fossdale Gill. After seeing the waterfall a few yards up, turn to accompany the beck downstream. A footbridge offers a choice of banks, and below two more low falls a second footbridge is reached. Here we must leave the beck to prepare itself for its big moment, to be witnessed from below: a path goes left up to join the road.

Go right for only a minute and leave the road by a stile alongside a gate. A good track heads away and down to West House Farm, and from a stile to its right a path descends two more fields to emerge via a yard into Hardraw. Access to the Force is through the inn, where a charge is made to view the 'private' spectacle: it is but a 5-minute walk into the increasingly impressive amphitheatre.

On returning to the inn, cross the road and take a track just left of the bridge. Behind the buildings go left to a small gate from where a good path crosses a series of fields to eventually join a road. Turn right to pick up the outward route, over Haylands Bridge and back into Hawes.

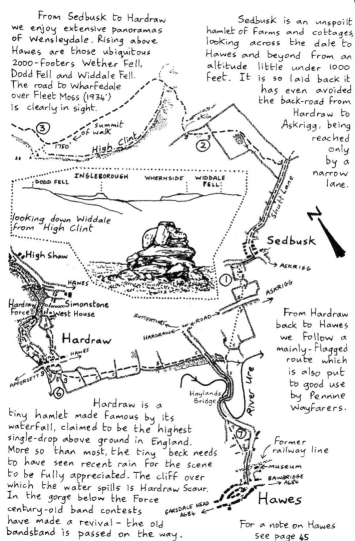

From Sedbusk to Hardraw we enjoy extensive panoramas of Wensleydale. Rising above Hawes are those ubiquitous 2000-footers Wether Fell, Dodd Fell and Widdale Fell. The road to Wharfedale over Fleet Moss (1934') is clearly in sight.

Sedbusk is an unspoilt hamlet of farms and cottages, looking across the dale to Hawes and beyond from an altitude little under 1000 feet. It is so laid back it has even avoided the back-road from Hardraw to Askrigg, being reached only by a narrow lane.

③ summit of walk 1750' High Clint

a kiln

②

INGLEBOROUGH WHERNSIDE WIDDALE FELL
DODD FELL

looking down Widdale from High Clint

High Shaw

HAWES

Hardraw Force

Simonstone West House

Hardraw

HAWES

APPERSETT

⑥

Sedbusk

ASKRIGG

①

ASKRIGG

BUTTERTUBS ROAD

HARDRAW

From Hardraw back to Hawes we follow a mainly-flagged route which is also put to good use by Pennine Wayfarers.

Haylands Bridge

River Ure

⑦

Former railway line

museum

BAINBRIDGE A684

Hawes

GARSDALE HEAD A684

Hardraw is a tiny hamlet made famous by its waterfall, claimed to be the highest single-drop above ground in England. More so than most, the tiny beck needs to have seen recent rain for the scene to be fully appreciated. The cliff over which the water spills is Hardraw Scaur. In the gorge below the Force century-old band contests have made a revival – the old bandstand is passed on the way.

For a note on Hawes see page 45

WALK 4

6½ miles

## CALDBERGH AND MIDDLEHAM LOW MOOR

from Coverham

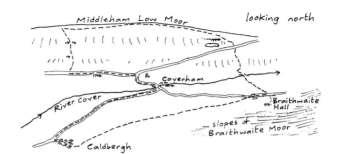

This leisurely ramble takes in several of lower Coverdale's interesting features

Parking can be found at the junction in front of the church, or down the lane just before the bridge

### THE WALK

Leave Coverham by crossing the bridge over the Cover and taking the quiet back road to Caldbergh. Turn up into the tiny village on a lane that terminates at the last of the houses. At a gate a farm track takes up the running, and is followed along to the left over several cattle-grids to arrive at Ashes Farm. A track then continues across the fields to cease at the second gate reached.

Carry on with a wall on the left, and at the next gate this too calls it a day. Continue straight across to a gate in a fence, then cross an extensive pasture by passing a plantation before gradually declining to the far corner, where a stile by a gate admits onto a road. Turn right on it, past a farm and along to the drive of Braithwaite Hall, with the familiar National Trust sign in evidence.

Opposite the drive is a gate, from where a track heads away on a steady descent to the river. The Cover is crossed by the stone-arched Hullo Bridge. From it a track bears left up the steep bank, an early right fork being the key to a sketchy but direct climb up a large

pasture. At the top a gate precedes the unfenced Coverham
- Middleham road over Middleham Low Moor.

Head straight up the opposite slope to join a wide
track which can be followed left to a wall-corner. It can
be rewarding to divert a little left off the track to enjoy
a bird's-eye view over the whole of Pinker's Pond. From the
wall-corner the track can be abandoned by striking a little
to the right across the largely pathless moor. This couldn't
be much less like the moors to which we are accustomed,
and the short-cropped turf is a joy to feel underfoot. While
keeping an eye open for racehorses the Ordnance column
soon appears ahead, and is equally quickly attained.

From the trig. point continue along the moortop's
broad crest a good while yet: the boundary wall on the
left remains in view for the most part, and on seeing the
first set of buildings behind it head in that direction. Do
not leave the moor here but accompany a wallside track,
and within a couple of minutes a solid drive is met. This
heads through a gate and down to the left, passing between
the buildings of Ashgill Stables and alongside the stables
of Tupgill to drop down the drive onto a road.

Turn left along the road, passing the sad shell
of a creamery of recent demise and soon arriving at the
junction at Coverham church. The right branch leads
straight back down to the bridge, but a visit to the church
can be incorporated by the lych-gate just ahead. A path
also leads from its right (south) side down onto the lane to
Coverham Abbey, which itself merits a look to conclude the
journey in fitting manner.

Coverham enjoys a sylvan setting at the lower end of
its dale, and is well and truly off the normal tourist
routes. Though barely even a hamlet it boasts several items
of interest. The abbey was founded by Premonstratensian canons,
and the scant remains
include 14th century
arches by a private
house. Also largely
defunct now is the
church of the Holy
Trinity, though the
old bridge still serves
its purpose.
The gatehouse

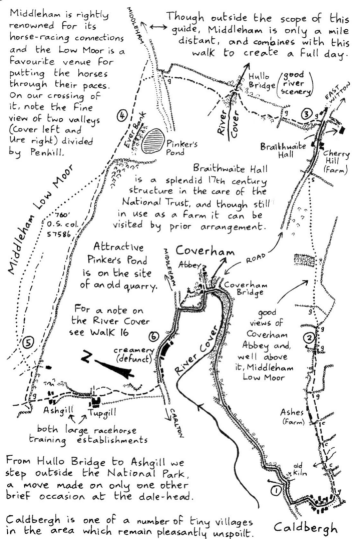

Middleham is rightly renowned for its horse-racing connections and the Low Moor is a favourite venue for putting the horses through their paces. On our crossing of it, note the fine view of two valleys (Cover left and Ure right) divided by Penhill.

Though outside the scope of this guide, Middleham is only a mile distant, and combines with this walk to create a full day.

Hullo Bridge (good river scenery)

Middleham Low Moor

760' O.S. col. 57586

Pinker's Pond

EAST WITTON

Braithwaite Hall

Cherry Hill (Farm)

Braithwaite Hall is a splendid 17th century structure in the care of the National Trust, and though still in use as a farm it can be visited by prior arrangement.

Coverham Abbey

ROAD

Coverham Bridge

Attractive Pinker's Pond is on the site of an old quarry.

For a note on the River Cover see Walk 16

good views of Coverham Abbey and, well above it, Middleham Low Moor

creamery (defunct)

River Cover

CARLTON

Ashgill    Tupgill

both large racehorse training establishments

Ashes (Farm)

old kiln

From Hullo Bridge to Ashgill we step outside the National Park, a move made on only one other brief occasion at the dale-head.

Caldbergh is one of a number of tiny villages in the area which remain pleasantly unspoilt.

Caldbergh

# WALK 5

## 6½ miles

from Worton

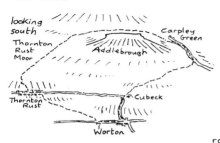

A straightforward circuit of this shapely fell, with outstanding views of the district

Park in the spacious lay-by opposite the inn, on the Aysgarth road out of the village.

## THE WALK

From the lay-by head past the inn to the first road junction, and turn up the steep lane to Cubeck. Turn into the farming hamlet and then immediately left up a steep, rough lane. At a gate the track runs more freely, sloping across a field and then up to a gate at the top corner. Behind it the track fades: cross to a gate over to the right after which the way picks up again to resume its level course. From the next gate it accompanies a wall away to emerge onto the quiet road to Carpley Green.

Turn left along its traffic-free course, leaving it only on approaching the first barn at the Farm. From a gate on the left follow a wall through a field to a gate giving access to a large pasture on Addlebrough's upper flank. A raised green way sets the course as it rakes across, bearing a little to the right to run roughly parallel with a wall down to the right, and then continuing on through a natural pass around the back of Addlebrough.

After two intervening walls the way finally links up with that right-hand wall and succumbs to a gate in it. An improving grassy track now surmounts a modest ridge, and beyond a stile the expanse of Thornton Rust Moor is firmly underfoot. Our splendid track strikes half-left across undulating terrain, leaving the moor at a gate from where walled confines channel us unerringly down into Thornton Rust.

Go left along the road to the edge of the village, and just past a cottage garden take a second small gate on the right, labelled *Nipe End*. From a stile below, a path runs through slender woodland to emerge into a field. Here the final leg begins, a pathless trek through green pastures linked by a fine collection of stiles. The only potentially confusing one is the first, found in the crumbling wall half-left of our emergence from the trees. This sets the general course for delivery onto the main road: the start is along to the left.

---

Addlebrough is a classic table-topped fell that seems to crop up in almost every Wensleydale view. Modest crags line its northern side, and help to accentuate the abrupt edge of the plateau. The Brigantes are thought to have occupied a hill-fort here - no doubt in stark contrast to the Roman fort in the valley bottom.

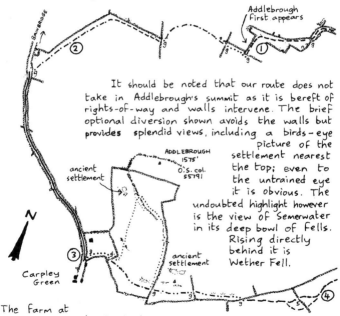

It should be noted that our route does not take in Addlebrough's summit as it is bereft of rights-of-way and walls intervene. The brief optional diversion shown avoids the walls but provides splendid views, including a birds-eye picture of the settlement nearest the top; even to the untrained eye it is obvious. The undoubted highlight however is the view of Semerwater in its deep bowl of fells. Rising directly behind it is Wether Fell.

The farm at Carpley Green stands at the end of the road as far as motor traffic is concerned, but an old packhorse way continues over the Stake to the Kidstones Pass and Wharfedale, a splendid route for walkers.

26

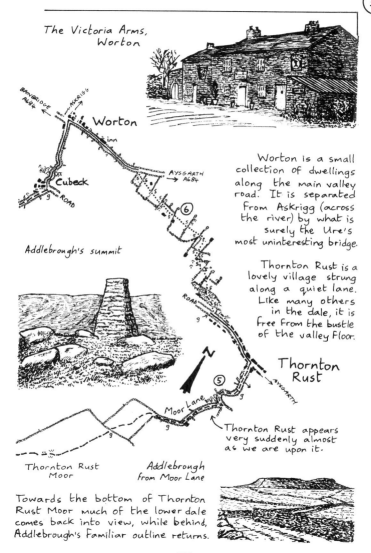

The Victoria Arms,
Worton

Worton

Cubeck

AYSGARTH
A684

(6)

Addlebrough's summit

Worton is a small
collection of dwellings
along the main valley
road. It is separated
from Askrigg (across
the river) by what is
surely the Ure's
most uninteresting bridge.

Thornton Rust is a
lovely village strung
along a quiet lane.
Like many others
in the dale, it is
free from the bustle
of the valley floor.

Thornton
Rust

(5)

Moor Lane

Thornton Rust appears
very suddenly almost
as we are upon it.

Thornton Rust
Moor

Addlebrough
from Moor Lane

Towards the bottom of Thornton
Rust Moor much of the lower dale
comes back into view, while behind,
Addlebrough's familiar outline returns.

27

# WALK 6

## IVY SCAR, CARPERBY AND THE URE

7¼ miles

from Aysgarth

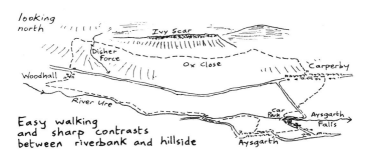

looking north

Ivy Scar

Disher Force

Ox Close

Carperby

Woodhall

River Ure

Car Park

Aysgarth Falls

Aysgarth

Easy walking and sharp contrasts between riverbank and hillside

Use the National Park car park at Aysgarth Falls

## THE WALK

Leave the car park at the opposite end to the entrance to find a well-used footpath leading down to Yore Bridge by the Upper Falls. Cross it and climb the steep road just as far as a stile on the right. An intermittent way runs across the fields, keeping generally level and squeezing through a multitude of identical gap-stiles on this villagers' church path. On the edge of Aysgarth the way becomes enclosed to join a back lane, which leads up to the Methodist chapel on the edge of the village green.

This is also the point where the village is departed, through a narrow gap between houses on the right. A path descends through two stiles and down alongside a wall, using a stile in it to cross half-right before arriving at an old mill. A stile to its left deposits us onto its access track, which is followed along to the left.

When the track turns to climb the hill, leave it by a stile on the right: beyond a barn another stile gives access to a pleasant path through trees by the riverside, emerging to continue on to a stile where road and river converge. Head on along the road for a very short distance to Harper Wath, where a long, narrow footbridge conveys us across the Ure.

A stile on the left marks the commencement of a long, easy stretch along the quiet riverbank. This pathless trek clings to the river to become temporarily confined in a rough section between an old railway embankment and the Ure. On emerging remain with the wall, crossing a small beck as the wall parts company before reaching a stile. Continue on to the next stile to join an enclosed farm track, and turn up beneath a former railway bridge. The improved lane rises up through the hamlet of Woodhall and out onto the Carperby-Askrigg road.

Cross straight over and pass between house and barns opposite to take a farm track up the steep field. Towards the top of the steep section opt for the right branch to the gate just ahead. The day's climbing is now complete, and a good, level track runs along to the right, through a gate to a ford at the top of Disher Force. While there is no right of way, a brief detour through the gate just before the ford provides a first-class view of this fine waterfall.

From a gate behind the ford, our track heads across Ox Close Pasture to the old lead mines under the shadow of Ivy Scar. Weaving through spoil heaps the track emerges at the far end to continue on its way a little sketchily. Eventually arriving at a gate, swing right to a gate – the second on the right – in the far corner, descending similarly a farm track through another field

Passing the remains of an old quarry the track falls to a gate on the right, continuing down through two fields. Halfway down the second locate a stile on the left, and cross a field-bottom to another stile. Descend the narrow enclosure to gates by farm buildings to emerge onto the road in Carperby.

Turn left along the main street as far as the inn, and take a gate opposite to enter a slender field in between houses. Keep on as far as a stile on the right, then continue on through a similar field to emerge via a stile onto a farm road, Low Lane. Cross straight over and follow a wall away to a stile on the right. From it an intermittent path strikes half-right through several fields, with a string of traditional gap-stiles serving to confirm the way.

Before long the path enters an attractive pocket of woodland: cross straight over the main track through it, and a path leads half-right down onto a road. Turn left, under the old railway bridge, and the Falls car park is immediately on the right. To round off the walk in style, a gate just across the road gives speedy access to the Middle Falls.

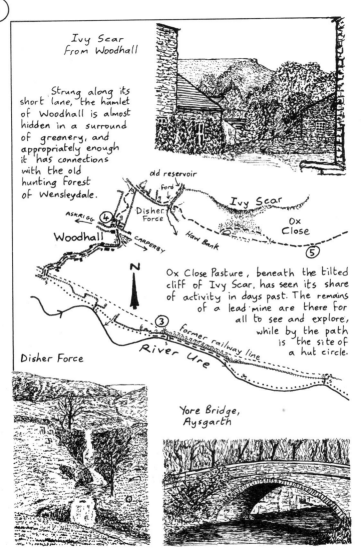

Ivy Scar
from Woodhall

Strung along its short lane, the hamlet of Woodhall is almost hidden in a surround of greenery, and appropriately enough it has connections with the old hunting forest of Wensleydale.

old reservoir
ford
Ivy Scar
Disher Force
ASKRIGG ④
Woodhall
CARPERBY
Haw Bank
Ox Close
⑤

N

Ox Close Pasture, beneath the tilted cliff of Ivy Scar, has seen its share of activity in days past. The remains of a lead mine are there for all to see and explore, while by the path is the site of a hut circle.

③ former railway line
River Ure

Disher Force

Yore Bridge, Aysgarth

The village of Aysgarth stands high above the river, and has a spacious air about it. A small green flanks the main road which divides the village. Aysgarth however stands quite aloof from the attraction that brings visitors in their tens of thousands to this corner of the dale, its famous waterfalls. Half a mile east of the village is the series of Upper, Middle and Lower Falls which make Aysgarth famous. Here the Yoredale series of rocks make their greatest showing to create a water-wonderland. It is the grand scale of things rather than their height that provides the spectacle. What makes all this truly *beautiful* is the setting — thickly-wooded with rich plant-life. The best viewpoint for the Upper Falls is Yore Bridge, a gracefully tall single-span structure. Originally from the 16th century, it has since been much-widened.

Yore of course is the older name for the river Ure.

For a note on Carperby see page 14

The large building adjacent to Yore Bridge is a former spinning mill, now being used to house the Yorkshire Carriage Museum. Up the steep hill behind is the parish church of St. Andrew. Restored last century, only the tower base of this very large church remains from medieval times. Inside are two fine 15th and 16th century screens.

To help complete the scene at Aysgarth Falls, one can also find an inn, a youth hostel, a gift-shop, a cafe and a National Park Centre at the car-park on the north bank

WALK 7

## THE ASCENT OF WETHER FELL

5¼ miles

from Burtersett

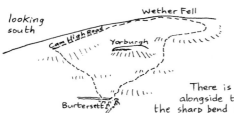

looking south

Wether Fell

Cam High Road

Yorburgh

Burtersett

A well-defined climb combined with a bracing stroll along a Roman road

There is reasonable parking alongside the lane just above the sharp bend at the village head

## THE WALK

From the tiny green at the top of the village, take the 'no through road' branching off the road corner alongside an old chapel. Almost at once it forks, and our track climbs to the left, leaving the last cottage behind and embracing a steep slope. This broad track still serves the farmer, and so remains easy to follow as it scales the hillside, always sloping to the right.

On gaining equal height with the highly prominent upthrust of Yorburgh just across to the left, ignore a right fork to a gate and continue straight up. Shortly afterwards the nearby wall finally leaves us for good, and the track —briefly a little less clear - crosses level ground to a gateway.

Beyond it the track improves again, winding up the fellside as a sunken, green way. Ignoring lesser branches to left and then right, the track arrives at the last gate of the climb. Ahead, set considerably well back, is the summit of Wether Fell, but the track heading directly out to it should be treated with contempt: within five minutes it will entice the hapless walker into dark, deep peat groughs — definitely not recommended.

Instead then, accompany the wall along to the right, passing an old quarry on Flint Hill and being greeted by new views across to the west. This rather more circuitous course should not be hastily abandoned: our thin path is heading ever nearer the top, and the temptation to strike out to the left is best avoided until the slope there becomes invitingly steep. At the same time as this our wallside way becomes marshier, less obvious and generally less appealing. Climbing

32

the grass to the left a few peat groughs are encountered at the top, and now the summit cairn appears only a couple of minutes beyond. A level, grassy stroll completes a relatively dry ascent.

To begin the return journey head down the only drop of any significance to join the broad track of the Cam High Road just to the south. This Roman road is now followed for quite a distance on its gentle descent eastwards to Bainbridge, soon becoming enclosed by walls. The point of departure from it is about a mile beyond this, where a footpath sign at a stile indicates the way to Burtersett.

A slender, green path slopes down to a stile from where a path slanting right is ignored in favour of the thinner one straight ahead. The path improves during a pleasant, direct descent of the large pasture to a stile just left of a wall-corner. Just a few yards over the brow Burtersett reveals itself, and the way is obvious through the final fields of the descent: from the bottom corner of a woeful plantation a trio of stiles precede emergence onto the road in Burtersett.

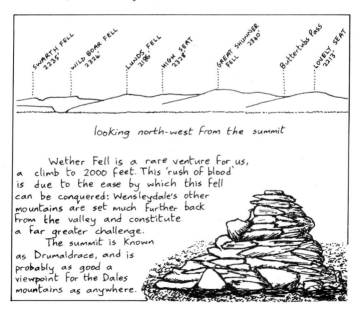

SWARTH FELL 2235'  WILD BOAR FELL 2324'  LUNDS FELL 2106'  HIGH SEAT 2328'  GREAT SHUNNER FELL 2340'  Buttertubs Pass  LOVELY SEAT 2213'

looking north-west from the summit

Wether Fell is a rare venture for us, a climb to 2000 feet. This 'rush of blood' is due to the ease by which this fell can be conquered: Wensleydale's other mountains are set much further back from the valley and constitute a far greater challenge.

The summit is known as Drumaldrace, and is probably as good a viewpoint for the Dales mountains as anywhere.

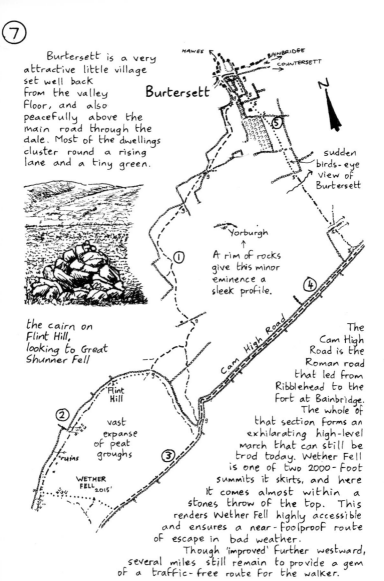

⑦

Burtersett is a very attractive little village set well back from the valley floor, and also peacefully above the main road through the dale. Most of the dwellings cluster round a rising lane and a tiny green.

HAWES

BAINBRIDGE
COUNTERSETT

Burtersett

N

⑤

sudden birds-eye view of Burtersett

Yorburgh
A rim of rocks give this minor eminence a sleek profile.

①

④

the cairn on Flint Hill, looking to Great Shunner Fell

Cam High Road

② Flint Hill

vast expanse of peat groughs

ruins

③

WETHER FELL 2015'

The Cam High Road is the Roman road that led from Ribblehead to the fort at Bainbridge. The whole of that section forms an exhilarating high-level march that can still be trod today. Wether Fell is one of two 2000-foot summits it skirts, and here it comes almost within a stones throw of the top. This renders Wether Fell highly accessible and ensures a near-foolproof route of escape in bad weather.

Though 'improved' further westward, several miles still remain to provide a gem of a traffic-free route for the walker.

34

WALK 8

7¼ miles

from Appersett

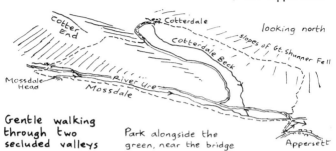

Gentle walking
through two
secluded valleys

Park alongside the
green, near the bridge

THE WALK

From the green cross the adjacent road-bridge
over Widdale Beck, and just beyond a barn take a stile
on the left. Walk parallel with the road as far as the
next bridge (this time over the Ure) but stay in the field
and cross a stile to follow the river up-dale. On emerging
from trees forsake the riverbank and slope up the field: pass
along the top of the trees, over a stile and across a hollow to
eventually reach a stile into the woods. Drop to cross a stream
entering the Ure, then head left to a barn, continuing straight
on to join the farm drive going left towards Birk Rigg.
        When it turns up to the farm, fork left on another
track through the gate in front, and accompany it through
four further gates. When it swings left to climb through a
low scar to Mid Mossdale Farm, leave it and head on to
the far end of the field. Now simply follow the river upstream,
past a farm bridge to a wedge of trees deflecting us from the
Ure. At a gate in the next substantial wall a sketchy track
strikes left to the now-prominent Mossdale Head Farm.
        Pass to the right of the main building to cross the
bridge over Mossdale Beck. From it ignore the various tracks
left and right, and instead climb the field with a wall on the
right. At the top go right over a stile in a fence, and stay
close to the right-hand wall as the declining slope steepens
to descend to the main road at Thwaite Bridge.
        Cross straight over both road and bridge, and head
up a path through the trees. From a stile at the top climb

35

the steep pasture to a stile at the top-right corner. Now continue over a gentler brow to locate a stile in the long wall climbing the ridge-end of the fell. From it cross to another wall, from where a steady descent - marshy in parts - can be made to the unfenced road in Cotterdale. Go left along the cul-de-sac road into the hamlet.

On approaching the last buildings leave the road by a footbridge, crossing the fields by obvious gap-stiles. A tiny watercourse takes us along a field-bottom, and at a collapsed intervening wall strike left up a pronounced green rake to a stile in the wall at the top.

Continued across - navigation.

continued across

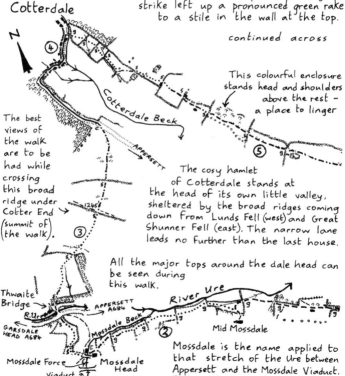

Cotterdale

N

This colourful enclosure stands head and shoulders above the rest - a place to linger

Cotterdale Beck

APPERSETT

The best views of the walk are to be had while crossing this broad ridge under Cotter End → (summit of the walk).

1245

The cosy hamlet of Cotterdale stands at the head of its own little valley, sheltered by the broad ridges coming down from Lunds Fell (west) and Great Shunner Fell (east). The narrow lane leads no further than the last house.

All the major tops around the dale head can be seen during this walk.

Thwaite Bridge
R. Ure
GARSDALE HEAD A684

APPERSETT A684
River Ure

Mossdale Beck

Mid Mossdale

Mossdale Force
Viaduct
Mossdale Head

Mossdale is the name applied to that stretch of the Ure between Appersett and the Mossdale Viaduct. Either side of the viaduct are some lovely falls. The 4-arch structure once carried the branch line from Hawes to Garsdale Head (then Hawes Junction) on the Settle-Carlisle line

Turn right to accompany the wall to a stile by a barn, and maintain this level course for some considerable time, through an assortment of pastures, sometimes with a wall for company, sometimes not. After a particularly clear spell the path becomes a little indistinct beyond the crumbling walls of an extensive fold. At the very end of the pasture rise to a gap-stile, then keep right of a short length of wall on a sheeptrod contouring round towards a stile above. From it contour yet again to join a broad track descending to a gate.

From the adjacent stile head down the enclosed track, only to leave it at the first gate on the right. Drop down by a wall to a stile, then head down to the far end of a large field. Shortly after the gate use a more prominent gate in the right-hand wall, then aim for a stile in front of roadsigns which indicate arrival at the Hardraw junction of the A684. Go left along the main road, crossing Ure Bridge and re-entering Appersett just as the walk began.

---

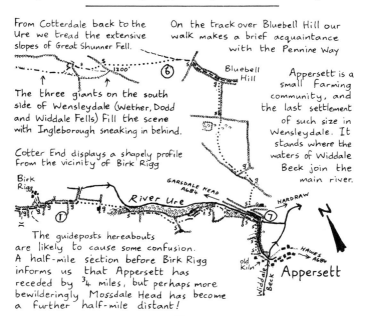

From Cotterdale back to the Ure we tread the extensive slopes of Great Shunner Fell.

On the track over Bluebell Hill our walk makes a brief acquaintance with the Pennine Way

The three giants on the south side of Wensleydale (Wether, Dodd and Widdale Fells) fill the scene with Ingleborough sneaking in behind.

Cotter End displays a shapely profile from the vicinity of Birk Rigg

Appersett is a small farming community, and the last settlement of such size in Wensleydale. It stands where the waters of Widdale Beck join the main river.

The guideposts hereabouts are likely to cause some confusion. A half-mile section before Birk Rigg informs us that Appersett has receded by ¾ miles, but perhaps more bewilderingly Mossdale Head has become a further half-mile distant!

WALK 9

6 miles

From West Witton

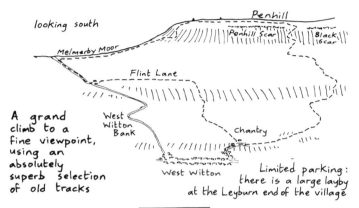

looking south

Penhill

Penhill Scar

Black Scar

Melmerby Moor

Flint Lane

A grand
climb to a
fine viewpoint,
using an
absolutely
superb selection
of old tracks

West
Witton
Bank

West Witton

Chantry

Limited parking:
there is a large layby
at the Leyburn end of the village

THE WALK

Leave West Witton by a lane at the west (Aysgarth)
end of the main street, by a small, grassy triangle of
land opposite the former school. Leaving the last of the
dwellings behind it climbs to a crossroads of ways: go straight
ahead and the lane becomes an enclosed track to rise past
an old quarry before arriving at a junction with a splendid
green road known as High Lane. Take the gate in front and
resume the rise on a green track, passing through two more
gates before emerging onto a plateau directly beneath the
cliffs of Penhill.

Our green path heads left before we fork away
from the wall to cross to the most distant of four prominent
spoil heaps. From it double back along the tops of the other
three, exploring as you go. At the last of these a path (one
of many hereabouts) rises just behind, and gently scales an
expertly engineered sunken way to the edge of Penhill's
summit plateau.

Turn left along the wall to a stile, continuing on
a sketchy path along the edge, passing the Ordnance column
over the wall before arriving at a small cairn. Just a few
yards further appears the mighty cairn on Penhill End.

Our descent over Melmerby Moor is well laid out below, as is an alternative bridleway through fields to the left. A path drops immediately away from the cairn to a stile in the wall-corner below, though various trods by-pass the steepness and thereby protect the vulnerable terrain. From the stile a good path remains close to the wall to cross the moor to the crest of the Melmerby-West Witton road.

Go left over the cattle-grid and down to Penhill Farm, after which turn left along an enclosed track known as Flint Lane. Its level course is trodden as far as a stile a short distance beyond a prominent clump of trees, from where a steep field is descended to a stile onto a similar green lane (High Lane again). From the stile opposite drop through two further fields onto a third and final green lane.

Turn left to a barn then bear right across the field behind to a stile. Be sure to peer over a fence ahead to see a waterfall in the wood, then take a wicket-gate to the left. A path crosses the caravan site at Chantry to leave by a similar gate, then descends steeply through trees onto the lane by which we departed the village. Go right, therefore, to re-enter West Witton.

---

Penhill is Wensleydale's best-known fell, its ability to stand out in views from afar outpointing its popularity as a climb. When its top is gained, it is usually by a quick stroll from a car at the top of Melmerby Moor. Its abrupt northern/north-eastern edge however renders Penhill as easily identifiable from most parts of Wensleydale, and it is a regular feature of views westward from the North York Moors.

Penhill's own virtues as a viewpoint are assisted by the dramatic plunge of the Scar, the top of which provides near-bird's-eye pictures of the lower dale. It is the aforementioned advantages which have given the hill historical significance. It was the site of a beacon, one of a chain throughout the land which when lit could rapidly spread the message of some impending danger. The coming of the Spanish Armada was of course top of the list. Something which is less certain is that this was also the location of an Iron Age chieftain's last resting-place.

Strictly speaking, the true summit of Penhill is a mile to the south-west of the Ordnance column, but an hour-long return plod is not recommended. To clarify what exactly is what on the summit plateau, the true top is over 1800', the O.S. column is at 1725', and the small cairn on the mound (the beacon site) is 1685'. To the east, and a little lower still is the big cairn on Penhill End.

West Witton is a pleasant village sadly split almost in two by the incessant traffic racing through. On the slopes of Penhill, it looks out across the valley from high above the river. The village is perhaps best known for an annual event here, the burning of Owd Bartle. An effigy, presumably of Saint Bartholomew to whom the church is dedicated, is joyfully burnt in Guy Fawkes fashion. The meaning of this seems to have gone up in the smoke of the years.

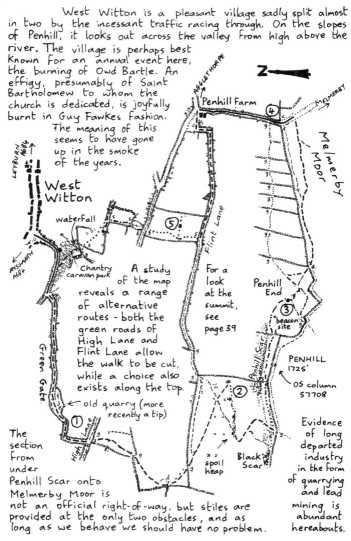

A study of the map reveals a range of alternative routes - both the green roads of High Lane and Flint Lane allow the walk to be cut, while a choice also exists along the top.

For a look at the summit, see page 39

The section from under Penhill Scar onto Melmerby Moor is not an official right-of-way, but stiles are provided at the only two obstacles, and as long as we behave we should have no problem.

Evidence of long departed industry in the form of quarrying and lead mining is abundant hereabouts.

# WALK 10

**7¼ miles**

## HELL GILL AND THE HIGH WAY

### From the Moorcock Inn

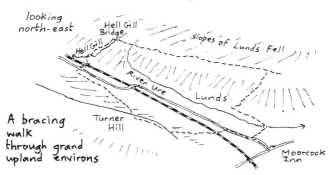

A bracing
walk
through grand
upland environs

There is ample parking in the vicinity of the inn at the junction
of the Kirkby Stephen road with the Hawes – Sedbergh road

## THE WALK

From the inn head down the Kirkby Stephen road
and leave it at a farm drive on the right bound for Yore
House. After crossing the Ure (choice of bridges) turn left
on a sketchy track upstream. Though it falters somewhat,
continue on to meet the drive to Blades as it bridges the
river, and follow it to the right.

At Blades pass between the buildings and at the
end take a gate on the right. A track crosses the field
to another gate, and a detour through two more gives access
to the steep pasture behind. When the sketchy way bears left
to a gate at the top follow it, maintaining this uphill course
to the derelict farm of High Dyke. Use gates to its right to
get onto the open fell.

Running alongside the intake wall is a track: this is
the High Way and it runs left on a generally level course all
the way to Hell Gill Bridge. For the most part the wall stays
with us, and when it eventually parts company the track runs
on to the top of a line of trees above a gorge. The way heads
on by small outcrops to quickly reach Hell Gill Bridge.

On crossing the bridge turn immediately left to
descend a track to farm buildings and then out along a drive.
With a railway bridge just ahead be sure to deviate right a

few yards for a dramatic appraisal of Hell Gill Force. Crossing the railway bridge the road is joined at Aisgill Moor Cottages.

Cross the road to a gate onto the moor and then follow the fence left to a wall. Though initially pathless the way is straightforward, with a wall, for the most part, for company. An occasional sketchy way runs on to the barns of High Shaw Paddock, shortly after which a large tract of rough pasture is entered. An intermittent path slants across to the head of a small beck before rising up above a marshy section to a gate in a fence.

Here we gain the long - and by this stage broad - ridge descending from Swarth Fell, and follow it left over the minor dome of Turner Hill. Continue down the wall-side to a stile by a gate, and from it vacate the ridge by descending the rather rough pasture on the left to a highly prominent footbridge high above the railway.

A track heads away to join the road, with the Moorcock only a few minutes along to the right.

Turner Hill is an excellent viewpoint, chiefly for the fine surround of fells. Besides a good stretch of railway, the best single feature is the entire length of Wensleydale stretching away.

Blades is the only farm we encounter which is still operating. The prominent white building on the hillside above-left is the former youth hostel.

High Dyke was once an inn catering for travellers on the old road.

The Moorcock's strategic position places it in that small band of well-known (from the outside at least) outpost-hostelries.

42

This walk is a real treat for railway enthusiasts, the famous line being visible much of the time. Just south of the cottages is Aisgill Summit, at 1169 feet the highest point on a main line in Britain.

This splendid waterfall makes a vertical drop over a cliff, and youngsters should be kept on a tight rein.

Aisgill Moor Cottages

KIRKBY STEPHEN B6259

CARLISLE

Hell Gill Force

④

GARSDALE HEAD B6259

SETTLE

N

Hell Gill Beck

Hell Gill

Hell Gill Bridge is a sizeable stone-built structure over an unexpected gem. The beck, source of the Eden, rushes through a deep, dark and narrow ravine. The old Yorkshire–Westmorland border (and modern equivalent) follows the beck down to the road. From the bridge to the cottages we make the only Wensleydale foray out of North Yorkshire, into Cumbria. In this area the National Park also shares the boundary.

High Shaw Paddock

Hell Gill Bridge

③

This last beck before Hell Gill Bridge is in fact the infant Ure here within 1½ miles of its birthplace on Lunds Fell. The rugged little gorge is one of its few lively moments outside of Aysgarth.

High Hall

The High Way

High Way

The "old Kiln"

②

The High Way is part of the route taken by Lady Anne Clifford on the way to her Westmorland castles. Now a route for more leisurely travellers, it once formed the major 'highway' through the valley.

*Wild Boar Fell (2324') from Aisgill Moor*

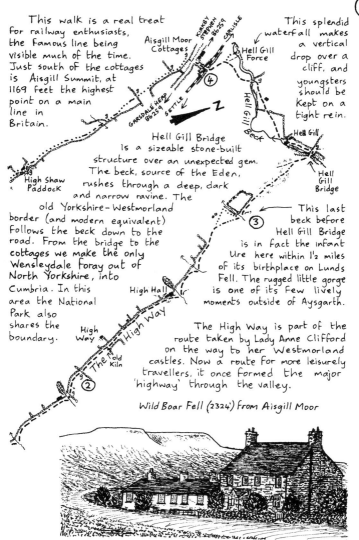

# WALK 11
## 3½ miles

### AYSGILL FORCE AND GAYLE

from Hawes

A simple stroll in the valley
of Gayle Beck

*looking
south-west*

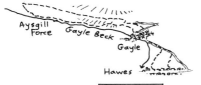

Use the main
National Park
car park in
the old
station yard

### THE WALK

Leave Hawes through the small main street car park almost opposite the Board Inn. From a stile in its left corner a sketchy path rises half-right across two fields to join the Gayle road. Turn left into the heart of the village, and after leaning on the bridge to survey the falls on Gayle Beck, take the short, cobbled way to the right, continuing along the lane to a kissing-gate after the last house on the left. Climb half-right past a wall-corner to a stile, and continue at the same angle to a stile above the beck before descending to its bank.

The way is now straightforward, shadowing Gayle Beck upstream to Aysgill Force. Above the waterfall remain with the beck past two footbridges, the second by a barn. At the end of the next field leave the beck by rising right to join a farm track at a gate. This green track now doubles back to the right, soon becoming enclosed and eventually gaining a solid surface. Just a little further, after a bend, a stile on the right commences our tracing of the Pennine Way into Hawes.

Firstly two fields are crossed to a stile used earlier in the walk, now turning left to accompany a wall down onto a lane. Almost immediately take another lane joining it to drop down onto the edge of Gayle. The Pennine Way avoids the village centre by branching left across two fields and passing between modern housing to debouch onto the road to Hawes.

Turn briefly left and then leave the road alongside a barn on the right. A flagged footpath runs on through two fields above Gayle Beck to arrive at the parish church. Either branch of the fork will safely deposit you back onto the main street in the centre of Hawes.

Hawes is the 'capital' of upper Wensleydale, a lively, colourful market town to which all visitors are drawn. The place gains even greater character at its Tuesday market, when there are, happily, as many locals in evidence as there are tourists. Hawes has retained an unconventional layout, including some cobbled road, and a leisurely exploration is really essential.

Once the last stop on the Wensleydale branch line, its station has been put to good use as a National Park Centre. Also keeping the station yard alive is the Dales Countryside Museum, where one can learn of local industries of which cheese-making is perhaps best known. Only yards away is an industry that is also a tourist attraction, the fascinating ropemaker.

Other places of interest include the parish church of St. Margaret; a modern youth hostel on this major staging post on the Pennine Way; and a celebrated antiquarian bookshop.

Note the profusion of field-barns above Gayle

N

old kiln

**Hawes**

GARSDALE HEAD A684
INGLETON B6255
HARDRAW → National Park Centre
BAINBRIDGE A684

creamery →
falls

③
BURTERSETT
BUCKDEN

**Gayle**

The delightful village of Gayle was here long before its big brother came on the scene. Its solid stone cottages fan out along lanes from the little arched bridge, on either side of which the beck tumbles over a series of ledges.

Gayle Beck
①
②

Aysgill Force

Deeply inurned in a wooded dell, this is one of the valley's lesser-known falls.

45

WALK 12

7 miles

Park in the centre of Askrigg

**NAPPA HALL AND ASKRIGG'S FALLS**

from Askrigg

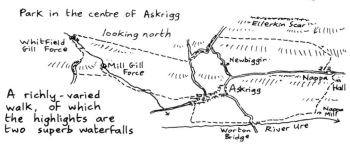

A richly-varied walk, of which the highlights are two superb waterfalls

---

**THE WALK**

Follow the main road in the Hawes direction out of the bottom end of the village, and after the last house on the left take a track down the near side of an animal feeds works. From the gate at the bottom pass between the ramparts of a former railway bridge and continue in the same direction through a series of stiles.

From the final stile a path heads straight on for the river, but instead of following it to the very bank, go left on a low embankment to a stile in a wall-corner. Follow the fence away from it (parallel with the Ure) to a stile by a gate, from where the riverbank is finally gained. Now accompany the Ure downstream to soon emerge onto a road adjacent to the characterless Worton Bridge.

Without crossing the bridge, continue down-river from a stile opposite. After a pair of footbridges in rapid succession a gate brings arrival at Nappa Mill Farm. Take the farm road up to the left, but leave it by a stile on the right just before crossing the beck at an attractive corner. Climb diagonally away on a green track up to the right-hand of two gates, and continue in the same direction to a gate admitting to the environs of Nappa Hall. Follow the enclosed track up past the farm buildings and out onto the road.

Turn left along the road only as far as the first branch right, signposted 'no through road', and head up through the hamlet of Nappa Scar. Remain on this lane which at the top of the hill becomes roughly surfaced: it now swings left for a long and hugely pleasurable level march to debouch onto a narrow road climbing out of Askrigg. Turn down towards the valley, ignoring in turn a road left, a track right, and then a road right (to Muker). Just below is another walled track, and this we follow along to the right.

Remain on this rough way known as Low Straights Lane to its very terminus, and here escape by a stile on the left: Whitfield Gill Force at once makes its presence known through the trees directly below. Our route must take a circuitous course in order to stand at its foot, for the steep slopes deter a direct descent. Instead the path heads downstream high above the wooded beck before dropping to a footbridge, then rises to meet the path to the waterfall. Turning upstream, care is needed as the final yards can be slippery underfoot.

To resume the walk retrace steps to the junction and keep straight on to a stile. From here on the original footpath spent much time outside the wooded confines of the gill, but a thoughtfully created replacement has provided us with a more intimate route. After a stile beyond a sidestream some time is still spent outside the boundary wall, but the path is soon returned to the action after the second of two sections in the fields.

The returned path runs once more along the top of the steep, wooded bank, and at a junction the detour to our second waterfall is made: the situation is a near-replica of the one experienced further up the beck. This time, however, it is but a brief stroll along a much firmer path upstream to witness the delights of the equally impressive waterfall of Mill Gill Force.

After admiring the cascades return to the junction of paths and continue downstream on an excellent path on the top side of the wooded gill. The bonus of a distant view across Wensleydale is now added to the charms of the gill itself. At the bottom of the wood a brace of neighbouring stiles point the way to a small footbridge on the beck.

Just downstream of the footbridge our track parts company with the beck to pass to the left of a former mill, and under a simple aqueduct to a stile. A neat, flagged path runs from here across the field to join a lane, which runs along to the left to re-enter Askrigg.

Askrigg is a wonderfully different village, seeming of another age to the 'typical' Dales village. Formerly a market town and a famous clockmaking centre, Askrigg gradually gave way to Hawes as centre for the upper dale.

The village centre still clearly recalls those days: the market cross, the three-storeyed houses along the main street and the 15th century St. Oswald's church with its splendid old beams. Flat-topped Addlebrough is prominent in the Askrigg scene.

Whitfield Gill Force

Although the two waterfalls occupy similar settings in deep wooded gorges, their characters are vastly different. The first is a straight drop, the latter a staircase of ledges.

Our brief meeting with the Ure finds it in predictably calm mood.

Askrigg's main street appears

This walk embraces such contrasting attractions that one may feel to be not doing justice to everything. More so than most the walk lends itself to being divided into two shorter rambles, using the Muker road as the link.

The outcrop up to the right here is Ellerkin Scar.

Above Nappa Scar the view becomes at once very extensive. The fells on the south side of the valley range from Penhill to Addlebrough, and Wether, Dodd and Widdale Fells.

Whitfield Gill Force

Mill Gill Force

Nappa Hall dates from the 15th century, a fortified manor house of the influential Metcalfe family. It now operates as a farm. Note the stunning carpet of snowdrops in the adjacent trees- in season!

WALK 13

6½ miles

## THE WALDEN VALLEY
### from West Burton

An intimate exploration
of an unfrequented
side-valley. Almost
gradient-free

*looking
south-east*

Park alongside
the village green
but *not* on the grass

## THE WALK

Depart the village green by a narrow lane on the left (ascending) signposted to 'Walden only'. When it forks take the left arm towards Walden South, and after a barn take a stile on the right. Here begins a long, largely pathless trek across the fields sloping down to Walden Beck. Mostly level, the ensuing amble requires little description: every intervening wall is graced with a stile.

The first deviation occurs after a good mile, when a wall deflects us half-right across a field with a beck in it. From the stile there cling to the perimeter of a fenced enclosure, beyond which a hand-gate precedes a footbridge over Cowstone Gill. Pass to the right of the house, over a stile, and head across the field to a gate opposite: through it a drive is joined to run along to Hargill Farm.

From the right-hand building cross the tiny beck to a hand-gate, and then resume a level march across the fields. Maintain this course through several more pastures before descending to the next farm, Bridge End. At this most distant point of the journey, take a stile a little beyond the buildings, then double back beneath them to a small farm bridge over Walden Beck.

On the opposite bank go immediately through a stile on the left, and continue downstream to a stile in a fence. Now forsake the beck by climbing half-right to a gate at the top corner. From it turn left to commence a long, level march complementing that of the outward leg.

Once more virtually pathless, the only difference on this section is that gates have largely replaced stiles. Before long the farm of Whiterow appears ahead: pass along the front of the buildings, from where its drive takes over to guide us out onto a lane. Turn left to follow its traffic-free course back down the valley, arriving at Cote Bridge over Walden Beck after a long mile.

Without crossing the bridge, take a gate on the right to accompany the beck downstream until reaching a footbridge over it. Once again forego the crossing, and this time head half-right away from it to a stile. Rise up the side of the next field to a stile halfway, then break across the field to an easily located gapstile. Now head straight across three further fields in a direct line: beyond this a track descends left, but we branch off it to a stile just before it reaches a gate.

Follow the left-hand wall around to reach the final stile, from where a path descends the edge of a field to a hand-gate on the left. Steps now lead down to a footbridge below West Burton Falls, which can be fully appreciated at closer range before turning right to emerge back into the village centre.

---

The Walden Valley is one of the least-known and least-changed in the Dales, and the reason certainly for the former, is that it is a dead-end for motor vehicles. Not only that, the quiet lanes that set off up each side of the valley fail to connect again, thereby denying any circular tour. The individual farms are the only settlements up-dale of West Burton. The beck flows a good 7 miles to reach the village, being born under the summit of Buckden Pike.

Cowstone Gill (Farm)

Walden Beck

Hargill (Farm)

Whiterow (Farm)

Bridge End (Farm)

map continuation overleaf

West Burton is an absolute gem of a village, not only well away from the main road through Wensleydale but also hidden from the lesser road that runs through Bishopdale to join it. Strictly speaking the village is in the Walden valley, and jealously guards the only entrance to it. Outstanding is the extensive green, with cottages stood back in appreciation. An obelisk of 1820 stands on market-cross steps, with village stocks nearby: 'round the back' are the delightful falls in a wooded dell.
This is surely Wensleydale's best!

**West Burton**

Just before reaching Cote Farm, note the scant remains of a chimney that was part of the Burton Smelt Mill, serving lead mines in the late 17th and early 18th centuries.

West Burton Falls

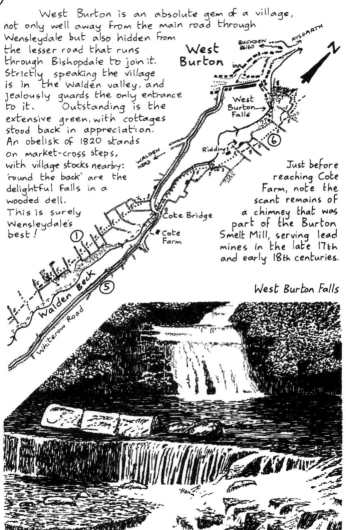

WALK 14 | REDMIRE FORCE AND THE TEMPLARS' CHAPEL

6¾ miles

from West Witton

looking
south

**Easy walking and easy
route-finding. Included
is the best long section
of riverbank in the valley**

The only parking is
along the main street, with
the best place being found
at the eastern end of the
village. Here there is a wide
verge just after the last
houses on the left. This is
also where the walk begins.

| THE WALK |

   At the east (Leyburn) end of the village take a walled
track just after the last house on the left. Almost at once it
forks, and here take the right-hand option. Twisting and turning,
the way leads steadily downhill towards the river, narrowing in
its latter stages. At its demise do not use the gate directly
in front, but opt for the gapstile by a gate on the right. In the
field adhere to the left-hand boundary wall until its various
indentations lead down to a gateway with the Ure now in close
proximity.
   Cross the stream behind and drop to a stile in the fence
to the right to gain the riverbank. Plain sailing now ensues as
the Ure is accompanied updale through a succession of quiet,
pleasant pastures. Eventually, beyond a large, wooded island and
a lively bend, a wall commences to separate us from the river.
Stay with the wall through a couple of fields, at the end of
which a stile admits to the thickly wooded bank. A path runs
through the trees, and almost immediately the splendour of
Redmire Force greets the eye.
   No sooner has the path deposited us alongside the
Falls then it is away again, forsaking the river by climbing
a stairway to a stile out of the woods. A generally straight

line now ensues through a succession of fields, all served by stiles. High above the wooded riverbank the route follows a fence to two neighbouring stiles, from where the fence heads across an extensive pasture. When it bends away, continue on ahead to a stile in the far corner.

A good path drops down through trees to briefly rejoin the river, but on emerging into a large riverside pasture we leave it for the last time. Following the wall curving away up to the left, a partially enclosed track materialises to lead onto the main road.

Being wary of the traffic, turn left up the hill to just short of Temple Farm, then take a stile on the right (good chance of mud here!) to follow a farm track running to the top end of the field. It enters a belt of woodland, and on emerging at the top a stile on the left gives access to the remains of the Knights Templars' Chapel.

A sketchy track rises to the top of the field, going on to join a concrete farm road. continued across

The Chapel of the Knights Templar is a little less exciting than it looks on the map. Here the low ruins of the chapel of the Penhill Preceptory include several graves, the structure itself dating from the early thirteenth century. Several adjoining buildings remained uncovered when this was excavated in 1840.

boundary post (Aysgarth/Leyburn) and also an inscribed stone similar to the one depicted, to be seen by the gate above the chapel.

here Penhill appears directly above, looking moody and menacing in the right conditions.

The roadside Temple (all very confusing this) was built in 1792 as a belvedere by the owners of nearby Swinithwaite Hall.

Follow the farm road uphill only as far as a bend right, then bear left up a vague track to the top of the field. From a gapstile in the angle of the wall head across a level pasture to a gateway, and with a wall on the right, follow it along to the terminus of a green lane.

This is Langthwaite Lane, and all is now very much plain sailing as this superb way is trodden all the way back to West Witton. Towards the end it meets a narrow road to descend into the village.

---

Despite being a major valley of the Dales, Wensleydale only attracts large numbers to its river at a very short stretch at Aysgarth. This much less-known section however provides outstanding company for several beautifully-wooded miles.

On descending Back Lane note the stately Bolton Hall on the opposite bank. Set in graceful parkland, this home of the Lords Bolton dates back three centuries.

in West Witton

For a note on West Witton see page 40

WALK 15

4 miles

SEMERWATER AND RAYDALE

from Semerwater

A very easy circuit of Semerwater.

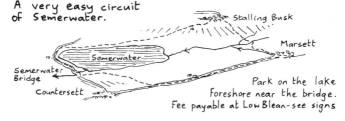

Semerwater
Stalling Busk
Marsett
Semerwater Bridge
Countersett

Park on the lake foreshore near the bridge.
Fee payable at Low Blean-see signs

THE WALK

From the foreshore head along the road away from the bridge (not over it), and at the foot of the hill - just opposite Low Blean Farm - take a stile on the right. Maintain a level course through the fields, taking in several stiles to emerge close to the lakeshore. By this time a good path has materialised, and it heads gradually upwards across the rough pastures above the head of the lake.

More stiles ensue before arriving at the remains of Stalling Busk's old church: a stile is provided to enable a look round. Only yards beyond it the barely evident path forks. Head up to the left on an improving path alongside a small beck: this old churchgoers' way leads unerringly up onto the cul-de-sac road through Stalling Busk.

Walk only a few yards to the right through the hamlet, and before a sharp bend take the rough track of Busk Lane down to the right. This enclosed way runs down to a ford at Cragdale Water, then heads away, forsaking it at a bend - by a footbridge - to cross two lesser becks directly ahead: this neighbourhood is usually rather moist. Beyond, the track soon becomes enclosed to enter Marsett alongside Marsett Beck.

Cross the green to the road bridge, and follow the quiet, generally level road for approximately one and a third miles. Shortly after a brief climb, journey's end beckons at the lakefoot, and as the lane descends take a stile into a field on the right. Accompany a tiny beck down to a gate, then crossing the beck to contend with a short, muddy walk through the trees. A gate admits onto the road at Semerwater Bridge, which is now crossed to complete the circuit.

Semerwater was the largest lake in the old North Riding of Yorkshire, and in a district not over-endowed with sheets of water it has become a popular venue for a variety of water-sports. An Association exists to control the activities and help protect bird-life. Near the lakefoot is the Carlow Stone, once dropped by a giant.

The best-known legend of the district relates how a visitor, inhospitably treated, caused a whole 'city' to disappear under the waters. What seems a little more certain is that Iron Age lake-dwellings existed here.

The old church at Stalling Busk stands in strange isolation some 200 feet below the hamlet. The ruins romantically overlook the lake, and exude an atmosphere not felt at the replacement St. Matthews up by the houses.

If one's boots should still be clean on leaving Marsett, a potentially squelchy finish can be avoided by remaining on the lane to the Countersett road-junction, and there turning right.

COUNTERSETT

River Bain

Semerwater Bridge

Carlow Stone

Low Blean

Semerwater

STALLING BUSK

Carr End

③

①

ruined church

Both Marsett and Stalling Busk are peaceful Farming hamlets, Marsett in the valley bottom and Stalling Busk perched on the hillside with good views of the lake.

N

BAINBRIDGE

Marsett Beck

Marsett

Raydale Beck

②

setts

Cragdale Water

Busk Lane

Stalling Busk

A cul-de-sac for motorists, but the start of a good walkers track over to Wharfedale

The side-valley containing Semerwater has no satisfactory name, though Semerdale has sometimes been offered as a makeshift title. Above the lake it is generally referred to as Raydale, this being the central, the largest and the only level one of the three valleys which merge between Marsett and Stalling Busk. Bardale and Cragdale are the lesser two.

## WALK 16

11 miles

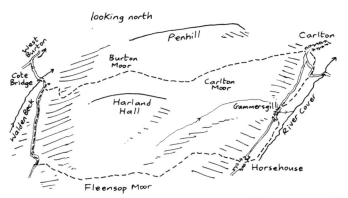

### OVER THE MOORS TO COVERDALE

from West Burton

*looking north*

An invigorating if mildly strenuous walk, using two fine inter-valley paths on high moorland to visit two Coverdale villages. Not surprisingly the views are extensive.

Take your sandwiches and make a day of this one!

There is reasonable parking just beyond Cote Bridge, which is reached from West Burton by the lane to Walden only. Fork left at the first junction and the lane descends to the bridge. If walking from West Burton, use the map in Walk 13 to reach and return from Cote Bridge. This adds an extra 1½ miles.

### THE WALK

Leave Cote Bridge along the lane running past Cote Farm and up the valley, and remain on its traffic-free course for about 1¼ miles. Above a steep rise a guidepost indicates the departure of a bridle-road to Horsehouse. Take this track to the left, passing through a gate and rising to swing left to a gate onto the moortop. Now virtually level a good path heads away, but after only a short way be sure to opt for the lesser left branch at a fork. It crosses the undulating moor to another gate, becoming very clear again to reach the headwaters of the Fleensop valley.

At another junction fork right to a gate, and after fording Fleemis Gill the track rises past grouse butts to a gate on the left. The last section of moor is crossed more sketchily to arrive at and follow a wall along to the left. Use the first gate in it to begin the descent into Coverdale. Head down the pasture, ultimately bearing left to a stile in the bottom corner, and make use of the walled confines of a wooded beck to drop into Horsehouse.

Turn right only as far as the inn, then take the lane running behind it for a short way to leave it by a white gate down to the right. Descend to the next gate, left to another and then cross to a hand-gate right of a barn. The river Cover is now joined and accompanied downstream for a mile. It is vacated at the end of the second enclosure after a pronounced wooded bend, crossing diagonally from the gate up to a red gate, and up again to a splendid stile well to the right of the buildings in view. A wooded enclosure leads onto the road through Gammersgill.

Go right along the road out of the hamlet, soon leaving it by a gapstile on the right. From it bear left to another stile to enter Turnbeck Lane, a delightfully narrow, green byway that is followed to its terminus. On emerging cross the field to a wall-corner and on again to the top far end of the next pasture. A beck is crossed to a well-hidden stile in the top corner: continue across to accompany a fence, using a stile in it to reach a stile onto a narrow road.

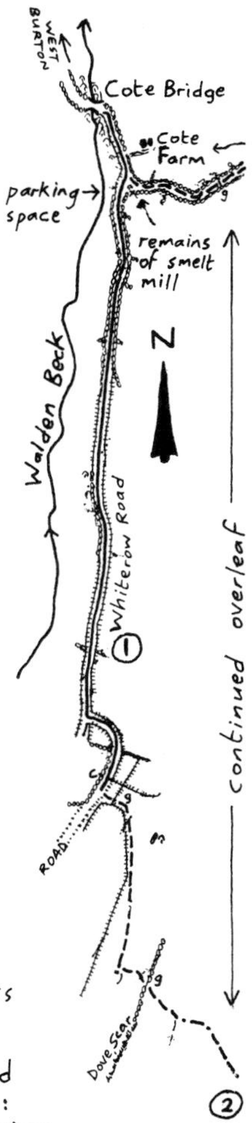

Head up this road (Cover Lane) just as far as the next bend, then take a stile to cross a field-bottom. From the next stile head for one in the top corner, then climb

**Map labels (right side):**

WEST BURTON

Cote Bridge

Cote Farm

parking → space

remains of smelt mill

N

Walden Beck

Whiterow Road

① 

ROAD

Dove Scar

② 

← continued overleaf →

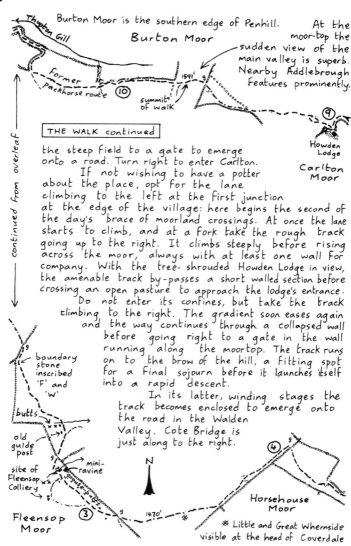

Burton Moor is the southern edge of Penhill.

## Burton Moor

Thupton Gill

At the moor-top the sudden view of the main valley is superb. Nearby Addlebrough features prominently.

Former Packhorse route

10

1591'

summit of walk

9

Howden Lodge

Carlton Moor

continued from overleaf

---

**THE WALK continued**

the steep field to a gate to emerge onto a road. Turn right to enter Carlton.

If not wishing to have a potter about the place, opt for the lane climbing to the left at the first junction at the edge of the village: here begins the second of the day's brace of moorland crossings. At once the lane starts to climb, and at a fork take the rough track going up to the right. It climbs steeply before rising across the moor, always with at least one wall for company. With the tree-shrouded Howden Lodge in view, the amenable track by-passes a short walled section before crossing an open pasture to approach the lodge's entrance.

Do not enter its confines, but take the track climbing to the right. The gradient soon eases again and the way continues through a collapsed wall before going right to a gate in the wall running along the moortop. The track runs on to the brow of the hill, a fitting spot for a final sojourn before it launches itself into a rapid descent.

In its latter, winding stages the track becomes enclosed to emerge onto the road in the Walden Valley. Cote Bridge is just along to the right.

boundary stone inscribed 'F' and 'W'

butts

old guide post

site of Fleensop Colliery

mini-ravine

N

4

Horsehouse Moor

Fleensop Moor

3

1470'

✳ Little and Great Whernside visible at the head of Coverdale

COVERHAM →

Penhill appears →

(8)

farm lane

Carlton

Carlton Moor

— Horsehouse —

ROAD

WEST SCRAFTON

(7)

N

Turnbeck Lane

ROAD

River Cover

ROAD

(6)

ROAD

High Gill

(5)

Horsehouse ↓ KETTLEWELL

↓ KETTLEWELL

Gammersgill is an untouched farming hamlet with a classic Norse title.

Coverdale is easily the longest of the Ure's many side-valleys: the sparkling River Cover joins the main river below Middleham. The road out of the valley-head leads over Park Rash to Kettlewell, and was part of the coaching route from London to Richmond. Earlier still it was used by visitors to Middleham Castle.

A famous son of the dale was Miles Coverdale, who first translated the Bible into English.

Gammersgill

Carlton-in-Coverdale (Sunday name) is one of the many linear villages in the district, and here the string of houses seems almost endless. There are numerous attractive cottages of a good age. On the south side of the village is the site of a castle of which little is known.

Horsehouse is the last sizeable community going up the dale. Here are pleasant grey buildings arranged in a compact huddle, including a cosy little inn and a modest church of 1869, dedicated to St. Botolph.

# LOG OF THE WALKS

These two pages provide an opportunity to maintain a permanent record of the walks completed

| WALK | DATE | TIME Start | TIME Finish | WEATHER | COMMENTS |
|------|------|------------|-------------|---------|----------|
| 1 | | | | | |
| 2 | | | | | |
| 3 | | | | | |
| 4 | | | | | |
| 5 | | | | | |
| 6 | | | | | |
| 7 | | | | | |
| 8 | | | | | |

| WALK | DATE | TIME Start | TIME Finish | WEATHER | COMMENTS |
|------|------|-------|--------|---------|----------|
| 9 | | | | | |
| 10 | | | | | |
| 11 | | | | | |
| 12 | | | | | |
| 13 | | | | | |
| 14 | | | | | |
| 15 | | | | | |
| 16 | | | | | |

## KEY TO THE MAP SYMBOLS

Route    ----clear----    sketchy    no path

Route on public road    wall   unenclosed   fence/hedge

Abbreviations   g = gate
s = stile   c = cattle grid

Railway line

Buildings    Church    Cairns   summit   other    Limestone clints

Crags    Loose rock /scree    Marsh    Trees

river or beck    tarn or lake    bridge    waterfall

Miles from start
③

Direction of North   N

Scale: approximately 2½ inches = 1 mile

---

### THE COUNTRY CODE

- Respect the life and work of the countryside
- Protect wildlife, plants and trees
- Keep to public paths across farmland
- Safeguard water supplies
- Go carefully on country roads
- Keep dogs under control
- Guard against all risks of fire
- Fasten all gates
- Leave no litter – take it with you
- Make no unnecessary noise
- Leave livestock, crops and machinery alone
- Use gates and stiles to cross fences, hedges and walls